Set the Table

Set the Table

11 Designer Patterns for Table Runners

Martingale
Create with Confidence

Set the Table: 11 Designer Patterns for Table Runners
© 2013 by Martingale & Company®

Martingale®
19021 120th Ave. NE, Ste. 102
Bothell, WA 98011-9511 USA
ShopMartingale.com

Printed in China

18 17 16 15 14 13   8 7 6 5 4 3 2 1

Library of Congress Cataloging-in-Publication Data is available upon request.

ISBN: 978-1-60468-321-9

Mission Statement

Dedicated to providing quality products and service to inspire creativity.

Credits

PRESIDENT AND CEO: Tom Wierzbicki

EDITOR IN CHIEF: Mary V. Green

DESIGN DIRECTOR: Paula Schlosser

MANAGING EDITOR: Karen Costello Soltys

ACQUISITIONS EDITOR: Karen M. Burns

TECHNICAL EDITOR: Rebecca Kemp Brent

COPY EDITOR: Melissa Bryan

PRODUCTION MANAGER: Regina Girard

COVER AND INTERIOR DESIGNER: Connor Chin

PHOTOGRAPHER: Brent Kane

ILLUSTRATOR: Christine Erikson

Contents

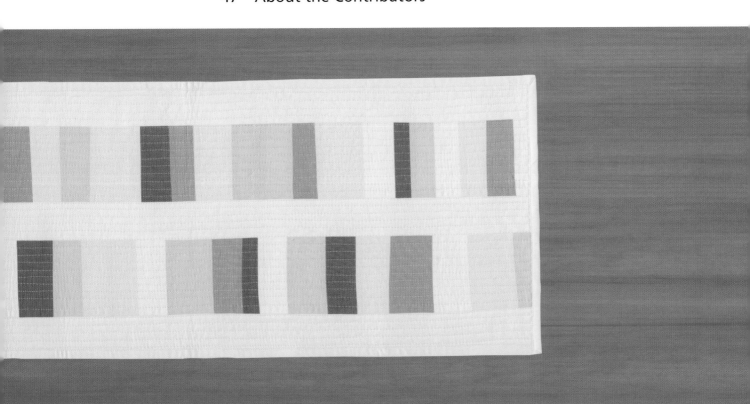

Introduction

Quilters love to make table runners. Whether subtle and sophisticated, bright and cheerful, or seasonal, a table runner will find a home on a dining table, coffee table, sideboard, wall, and anywhere else a quilter can put a long, skinny quilt.

Is it the shape that makes them so appealing? Perfect for gracing a table, of course, a table runner also can be just the thing to fill an awkward space beside a door or in a narrow hallway, or add a bright accent to the foot of a bed.

Maybe it's the scale of the project that draws people in. With a smaller investment of time, money, and energy than the average quilt requires, you can produce a stunning accent for your home or a much-appreciated gift. What an impressive way to say "Thank you," "Congratulations on your new home," or "Merry Christmas"!

Or maybe it's the chance to experiment with a new technique, play with color and design, or indulge in some simple, stress-free sewing that makes table runners so popular. Whatever the attraction, their popularity never seems to wane.

We asked a group of outstanding designers if they'd like to contribute a pattern to our new collection, and guess what: they all said yes! Because quilters *love* to make table runners!

The projects in these pages reflect the exciting diversity in quiltmaking today. Bold, graphic design? Check. Traditional blocks reinterpreted? Check. Solid fabrics, simple shapes, and amazing quilting? Check, check, and check. Oh, and a lineup of designers that reads like a mini who's who of quilt bloggers.

Are you ready to get started? Just turn the page and start browsing. You're sure to find a project (or three) that speaks to you. Have fun!

Mary Green

Mary V. Green
Editor in Chief

Using Precuts

With their small size, table runners are great projects for incorporating fat quarters (18" x 21") and fat eighths (9" x 21"). Project instructions will specify these precut units when appropriate. If your fat eighth is cut 10" x 18", adjust the cutting instructions accordingly.

Confetti

Natalie has some wonderful friends who organized a celebratory lunch for her most recent birthday. When she walked into the restaurant, her friends announced, "It's her birthday!" Then they led her to a table that was decorated down the center with a colorful sprinkling of confetti. Natalie decided to make her own "Confetti," not only to remember that special day with special people, but to transform her own table into a celebration.

Designed and made by Natalie Barnes

Finished runner: 12" x 72"   **Finished block:** 12" x 12"

Materials

Yardage is based on 42"-wide fabric except as noted.

17 strips, 2½" x 42", of assorted dark-purple, green, and burgundy prints for blocks

3 fat quarters *OR* 6 strips, 2½" x 42", of assorted bright orange or red accent prints for blocks

⅜ yard of purple batik for binding

1¼ yards of fabric for backing

18" x 78" piece of batting

Let the Fabric Do the Work

The seemingly random design in this runner is constructed from four-patch units incorporated into Nine Patch blocks. The "confetti" is all in the color placement, so choose colorful fabrics with high contrast. Natalie used 2½"-wide Bali Pops strips from Hoffman California for the bright, saturated colors in this project.

Cutting

All dimensions include ¼"-wide seam allowances.

From 12 of the assorted dark strips, cut *a total of*:
162 squares, 2½" x 2½"

From the 5 remaining dark strips:
Trim each strip to 1½" x 42"; crosscut a total of 108 squares, 1½" x 1½"

Continued on page 10.

From *each* of the 3 bright accent prints, cut:

    1 strip, 2½" x 21"; crosscut *a total of* 18 squares, 2½" x 2½"

    2 strips, 1½" x 21"; crosscut *a total of* 36 squares, 1½" x 1½"

From the binding fabric, cut:

    5 strips, 2" x 42"

Flexible Placement

If desired, make extra four-patch units to allow flexibility for creating completely random blocks. Use the leftover pieces to make coordinating coasters.

Making the Blocks

Each 12½" x 12½" block is composed of nine four-patch units, and each four-patch unit includes one piece of bright accent print for confetti. There are three different four-patch layouts, designated blocks A, B, and C; you'll make 18 of each. To prepare for piecing the blocks, stack the fabrics by your sewing area.

1 Lay out a small four-patch unit using three 1½" dark squares and one 1½" bright square. Sew the squares together in two rows. In the row with one bright and one dark square, press the seam allowances toward the dark fabric; in the row with two dark squares, press the seam allowances in the other

direction so that the seams will nest together. Repeat to make 36 four-patch units.

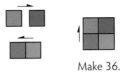

Make 36.

2 To make block A, join one small four-patch unit and three assorted 2½" dark squares as shown. Repeat to make 18 of block A. Press. The blocks should measure 4½" x 4½".

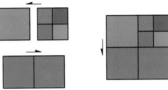

Block A.
Make 18.

3 To make block B, join one small four-patch unit and three assorted 2½" dark squares as shown. This is similar to block A, but the placement of the bright square is different. Press. Repeat to make 18 of block B. The blocks should measure 4½" x 4½".

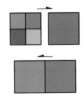

Block B.
Make 18.

4 To make block C, join three assorted 2½" dark squares and one 2½" bright square as shown. Make 18 of block C. The blocks should measure 4½" x 4½".

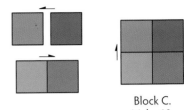

Block C.
Make 18.

5 Join three each of blocks A, B, and C to create a 12½" Nine Patch block, placing the A blocks on the left, the B blocks on the right, and the C blocks in the center. Lay out the first row as shown, and then rotate the A, B, and C blocks 90° for the next row. Repeat for the third row, as shown.

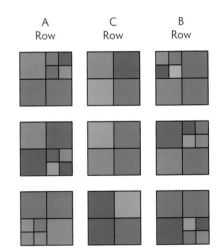

A Row   C Row   B Row

6 Sew the A, B, and C blocks together in rows, matching all seam intersections. Pin for accuracy, removing pins as you sew. Press. Sew the three rows together to complete the Nine Patch block. Make six.

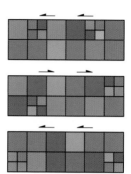

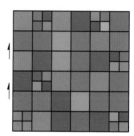

Make 6.

Assembling the Table Runner

Lay out the six large blocks as shown at right, rotating each block 90° from the previous block to create the random effect shown in the sample table runner. When you're satisfied with the layout, sew the blocks together and press.

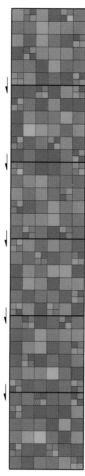

Table-runner assembly

Finishing the Table Runner

For more details on any of the finishing techniques, go to ShopMartingale.com /HowtoQuilt for free download-able information.

1 Cut two rectangles, 20" x 45", from the length-wise grain of the backing fabric. Sew the two pieces together along the short edges; press the seam allowances open.

2 Layer the table-runner top, batting, and backing; baste the layers together. Quilt as desired.

3 Trim the backing and batting to match the table-runner top.

4 Join the 2" x 42" binding strips and bind the table runner. Add a label if desired.

Choosing a Quilting Motif

When looking for a quilt-ing motif, Natalie often goes right to the fabric in the quilt. The zigzag quilt-ing that completes her table runner came directly from one of the batiks she used. Another handy tip: Use any leftover blocks from your runner to test the quilting motif, thread colors, and tension. This gives you a chance to make sure you like your choices before quilting the finished project.

Jewel Chain

This table runner is made from the simple, traditional Jewel Box block; stitched in irresistible fabrics, the block becomes fun and new again. The jewel-tone fabrics against a light-gray background create an illusion of sparkling gems that will brighten any table.

Designed and pieced by Audrie Bidwell; quilted by Laura McCarrick

Finished runner: 17" x 65"   Finished block: 12" x 12"

Materials

Yardage is based on 42"-wide fabric except as noted.

1⅛ yards of light-gray solid for blocks and border

10 fat eighths of assorted jewel-tone prints for blocks and binding

1¼ yards of fabric for backing*

23" x 71" piece of batting

To avoid a seam in the backing, purchase 2 yards of fabric.

Cutting

All dimensions include ¼"-wide seam allowances.

From the light-gray solid, cut:
> 5 strips, 2" x 42"; crosscut into 10 strips, 2" x 18"
>
> 3 strips, 4" x 42"; crosscut into 20 squares, 4" x 4"
>
> 4 strips, 3" x 42"

From *each* of the jewel-tone fat eighths, cut:*
> 1 strip, 2" x 18"
>
> 1 strip, 2½" x 19"
>
> 2 squares, 4" x 4"

Refer to the cutting diagram at right to make best use of fabric.

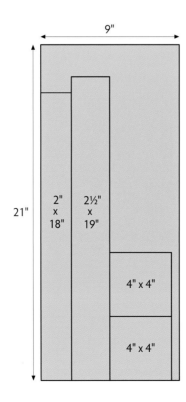

Making the Blocks

The blocks are composed of four-patch units and half-square-triangle units.

Four-Patch Units

1 Sew a 2" x 18" jewel-tone strip to a 2" x 18" light-gray strip. Press the seam allowances toward the darker fabric. Repeat to make a total of 10 strip sets. Cut eight 2"-wide segments from each strip set, for a total of 80.

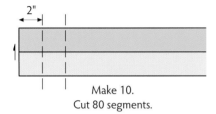

Make 10.
Cut 80 segments.

Straightening Segments

The strip sets are a little longer than necessary, so check the straightness of the cut after every three or four segments and make a "cleanup cut" if needed. Use ruler markings to make sure the cut edge is perpendicular to the seam line of the strip set.

2 Pair the strip-set segments to make 40 four-patch units and sew. Press the seam allowances in one direction.

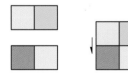

Make 40.

Seams Right

If you prefer to have the center seams of the four-patch units running in the same direction throughout the project, assemble mirror-image four-patch units, 20 of each.

Half-Square-Triangle Units

1 Draw a diagonal line from corner to corner on the wrong side of each 4" light-gray square. Pair a gray square with each 4" jewel-tone square, right sides together. Sew ¼" from the line on each side as shown.

Sew.

2 Cut along the drawn line and press the seam allowances toward the darker fabric. Trim each half-square-triangle unit to measure 3½" x 3½". Make 40.

Cut.   Press.
         Make 40.

Take Time to Trim

As you finish each four-patch and half-square-triangle unit, take time to square it up to 3½" x 3½" to achieve a beautiful runner top.

Assembling the Blocks

1 To make the Jewel Box block, arrange eight half-square-triangle units and eight four-patch units as shown below. Sew the units together in rows and press the seam allowances in opposite directions in alternate rows.

2 Sew the rows together and press the seam allowances in one direction.

3 Repeat to make five Jewel Box blocks.

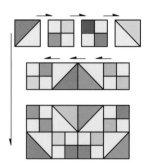

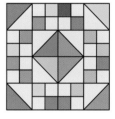

Make 5.

Assembling the Table Runner

1 Sew the Jewel Box blocks together. Press the seam allowances in one direction.

2 Sew two 3" x 42" light-gray strips together end to end. Cut one 60½" length and one 17½" length from the assembled strip. Repeat with the two remaining 3" x 42" light-gray strips.

3 Stitch a 60½"-long strip to each long edge of the table runner and press the seam allowances toward the border strips.

4 Attach the 17½"-long strips to the ends of the table runner and press the seam allowances toward the border strips.

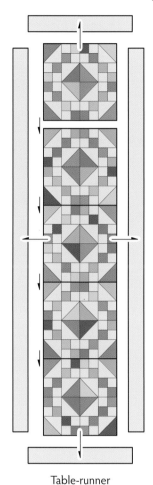

Table-runner assembly

Finishing the Table Runner

For more details on any of the finishing techniques, go to ShopMartingale.com /HowtoQuilt for free downloadable information.

1 Cut the backing fabric in half to make two 22½" pieces. Remove the selvages and sew the two pieces together along the short edges; press the seam allowances open.

2 Layer the table-runner top, batting, and backing; baste the layers together. Quilt as desired.

3 Trim the backing and batting to match the table-runner top.

4 Join the 2½" x 19" jewel-tone strips and bind the table runner. Add a label if desired.

Stand Out

Playing with value and contrast is a great way to achieve a contemporary look while using only solid-color fabrics.

Designed and made by Josée Carrier
Finished runner: 12½" x 48"

Materials

Yardage is based on 42"-wide fabric.

½ yard of gray solid for background

⅜ yard of eggplant solid for patchwork and binding

⅛ yard *each* of 4 yellow solids in different values (from light to dark) for patchwork

1½ yards of fabric for backing

18" x 54" piece of batting

Cutting

All dimensions include ¼"-wide seam allowances.

From the gray solid, cut:
2 rectangles, 4½" x 12½"
1 rectangle, 12½" x 22"

From the eggplant solid, cut:
4 strips, 2½" x 42"
2 squares, 2" x 2"

From *each* of the yellow solids, cut:
24 squares, 2" x 2" (96 total; you will have 2 left over)

Making the Blocks

1 Divide the assorted yellow squares into two groups of 48 each. On a design wall or other flat surface, arrange the groups into six rows of eight squares each to form two blocks. The arrangements should have a somewhat random effect, but take care to distribute the assorted yellows evenly, avoiding adjacent squares of the same shade. In one block, replace the yellow square in the fourth row, third column with an eggplant square. In the other block, substitute an eggplant square in the third row, sixth column.

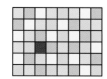 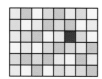

2 Working in rows, chain
piece the squares together
in pairs; join the pairs to form
complete rows. Press the seam
allowances in alternating directions from row to row.

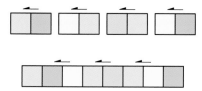

3 Sew the rows together to
make two patchwork
blocks. Press the seam allowances to one side.

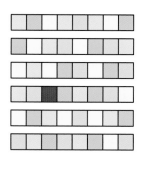

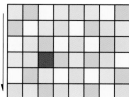

Assembling the Table Runner

1 Sew a 4½" x 12½" gray
rectangle to one side of
each patchwork block.

2 Sew the assembled units
to the short ends of the
12½" x 22" gray rectangle. Press
the seam allowances toward
the gray fabric.

Table-runner
assembly

Finishing the Table Runner

For more details on any of the
finishing techniques, go to
ShopMartingale.com
/HowtoQuilt for free downloadable information.

1 Cut an 18" x 54" rectangle
of backing fabric.

2 Layer the table-runner top,
batting, and backing;
baste the layers together. Quilt
as desired.

3 Trim the backing and
batting to match the table-
runner top.

4 Join the 2½" x 42" egg-
plant strips and bind the
table runner. Add a label if
desired.

Shake Up

A fascination with the year 1969—a time of generational conflict, social transformation, and cultural upheaval—led to this project. This table runner takes two iconic but very different objects from that period—the martini shaker and the Lava Lamp—as inspiration for a dynamic interplay of positive and negative space. The different forms coming together echo the mingling of generations and viewpoints around a dining-room table at the holidays.

Designed and pieced by Thomas Knauer; quilted by Lisa Sipes
Finished runner: 18" x 64"

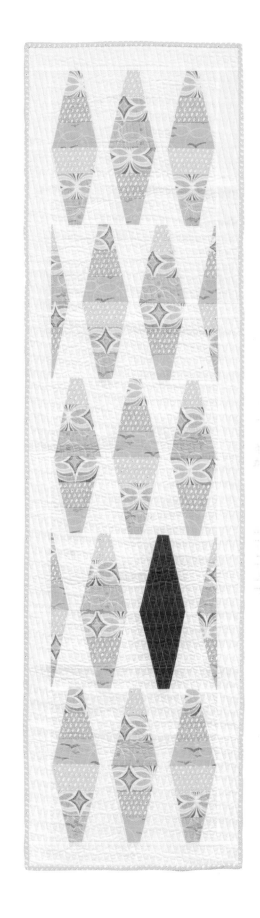

Materials

Yardage is based on 42"-wide fabric.

1 yard of white solid for patchwork and border

¼ yard *each* of 6 assorted prints for patchwork

1 rectangle, 6½" x 8", of dark-brown solid for patchwork

⅜ yard of gold print for binding

1⅜ yards of fabric for backing

24" x 70" piece of batting

Template plastic

Cutting

All dimensions include ¼"-wide seam allowances.

From the white solid, cut:
    3 strips, 6½" x 42"
    5 strips, 2½" x 42"

From *each* of the assorted prints, cut:
    2 strips, 2½" x 42"

From the gold print, cut:
    5 strips, 2½" x 42"

Making the Patchwork Units

1 Sew three assorted 2½" print strips together to create a strip set. Make a second, identical strip set. Repeat to make two identical strip sets from the remaining print strips, for a total of four strip sets.

2 Make a plastic template of the pattern on page 22. Use it to trace and then cut 14 pieces from each strip-set color combination, rotating the template 180° after each cut. You should have seven A units and seven B units of *each* color combination.

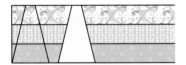

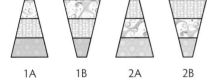

| 1A | 1B | 2A | 2B |

3 Cut one of each of the four types of strip-set units in half vertically; these will be used for the half shakers along the runner edges.

Cut.

4 Use the template to cut two shapes from the dark-brown rectangle and 30 shapes from the 6½"-wide white strips. Cut six of the white units in half vertically.

Assembling the Table Runner

The runner top is pieced in rows, alternating white and strip-pieced units.

1 Lay out the strip-set units and solid pieces to create the quilt top. The 1A units combine with 2B units to make shaker 1, and the 2A and 1B units make shaker 2. Alternate shakers 1 and 2 in the runner, inserting the dark-brown shaker into the fourth row.

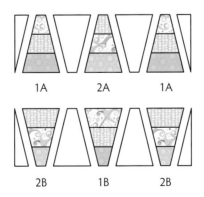

| 1A | 2A | 1A |
| 2B | 1B | 2B |

2 Sew the units together in half rows as shown. Sew the top and bottom halves of each row together. Make three rows with three shakers each, and two rows with two full and two half shakers each.

Make 3.

Make 2.

3 Join the rows to make the table runner. Press the seam allowances in the same direction.

Adding the Border

1 Remove the selvages and sew two 2½" x 42" white strips together end to end. Press the seam allowances open. Make two.

2 Measure the length of the pieced table runner through the center and cut one strip that length from each assembled border strip. Sew the strips to the long edges of the table runner. Press the seam allowances toward the border strips.

3 Measure the width of the runner through the center, including the side borders just added. Cut two strips that length from the remaining 2½"-wide white strip. Sew the strips to the short ends of the table runner. Press the seam allowances toward the border strips.

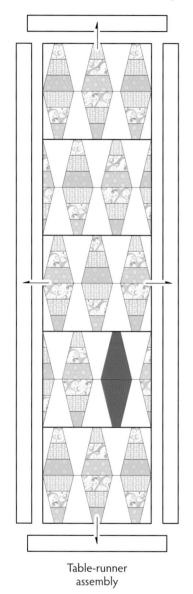

Table-runner
assembly

Finishing the Table Runner

For more details on any of the finishing techniques, go to ShopMartingale.com /HowtoQuilt for free downloadable information.

1 Cut two rectangles, 24" x 42", from the backing fabric. Remove the selvages and sew the two pieces together along the short edges; press the seam allowances open.

2 Layer the runner top, batting, and backing; baste the layers together. Quilt as desired.

3 Trim the backing and batting to match the table-runner top.

4 Join the 2½" x 42" gold strips and bind the table runner. Add a label if desired.

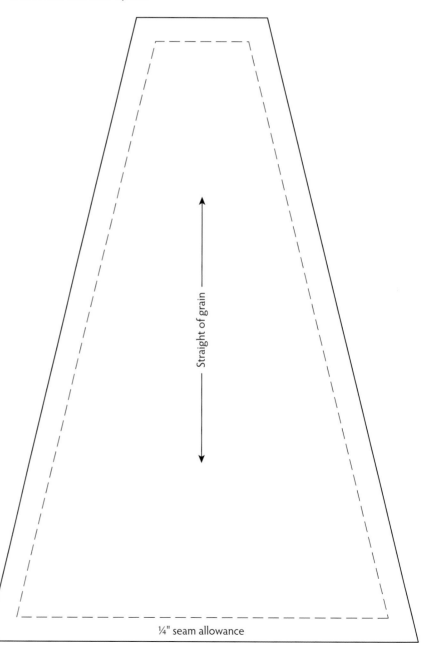

Straight of grain

¼" seam allowance

Improv Stripes

Improv, or improvisational, quilting leads to the creation of highly individualized, one-of-a-kind projects. This table runner is a great way to start working in an improvised manner, and the result will truly be an expression of your unique style.

Designed and made by Heather Jones
Finished runner: 14" x 36"

Materials

Yardage is based on 42"-wide fabric.

¾ yard of light-cream solid for piecing, sashing, and binding

¼ yard *each* of pale-blue, dark-gray, dark-cream, and taupe solids for piecing

½ yard of fabric for backing

20" x 42" piece of batting

Cutting

All dimensions include ¼"-wide seam allowances.

From the light-cream solid, cut:
  1 strip, 6" x 42"; crosscut into a variety of rectangles and wedges from 1½" to 3" wide*
  3 strips, 2½" x 36½"
  3 strips, 2½" x 42"

From *each* of the remaining solids, cut:
  1 strip, 6" x 42"; crosscut into a variety of rectangles and wedges from 1½" to 3" wide*

See "Relax" below.

Relax

Don't worry about precise measurements of the rectangles as you cut. The key to improv piecing is using randomly sized rectangles; the only thing that must be consistent is their 6" height. To add more visual interest to the project, cut some of the rectangles at a slight angle, forming wedges.

The cutting instructions include extra pieces, allowing you to more easily achieve a random color arrangement. Keep the leftovers for another project.

Making the Rows

1 Arrange the rectangles and wedges randomly into two rows. Position the angled wedges so that the rows are fairly straight overall. Sew the pieces together to create strips at least 38" long.

2 Press the seam allowances open and trim each strip to 4½" x 36½".

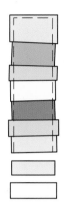

Assembling the Table Runner

1 Sew a 2½" x 36½" light-cream strip to each long edge of one improv strip. Press the seam allowances toward the sashing strips.

2 Sew the remaining 2½" x 36½" light-cream strip to one long edge of the second improv strip. Press the seam allowances toward the sashing.

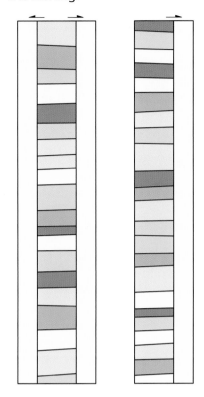

✗ Quilting with a Walking Foot

In her table runner, Heather quilted straight lines approximately ⅜" apart using a walking foot. This specialty foot comes in handy for straight-line quilting because it helps move all the layers of fabric and batting through the machine at the same rate, reducing the likelihood of puckering during the quilting process. If your machine didn't come with a walking foot, be sure to purchase one that fits your machine's brand and model.

3 Join the two sections to complete the table-runner top. Press the seam allowances toward the sashing.

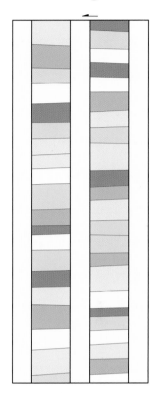

Table-runner assembly

Finishing the Table Runner

For more details on any of the finishing techniques, go to ShopMartingale.com /HowtoQuilt for free downloadable information.

1 Cut a 20" x 42" rectangle from the backing fabric.

2 Layer the table-runner top, batting, and backing; baste the layers together. Quilt as desired.

3 Trim the backing and batting to match the table-runner top.

4 Join the 2½" x 42" light-cream strips and bind the table runner. Add a label if desired.

Calamity Cross

The easy little block in this table runner was the result of random experimentation. Jenifer made a simple bordered-square block, sliced it in two, and added a darker strip. She then cut it in two again and added a second strip to make a cross. Voilà! You end up with a fun block, without the fuss of cutting and sewing lots of small pieces.

Designed and made by Jenifer Dick
Finished runner: 12" x 72"   **Finished block:** 6" x 6"

Materials

Yardage is based on 42"-wide fabric.

2¼ yards of yellow solid for blocks, background, binding, and backing

¼ yard of cream solid for blocks

¼ yard of dark-gold solid for blocks

18" x 78" piece of batting

Cutting

All dimensions include ¼"-wide seam allowances.

From the yellow solid, cut on the *lengthwise* grain:
   1 strip, 5½" x 72½"
   1 strip, 1½" x 72½"
   1 strip, 18" x 78"
   3 strips, 2" x 72"

From the remainder of the yellow solid, cut on the *crosswise* grain:
   10 rectangles, 1½" x 3½"
   12 rectangles, 1½" x 6½"
   10 rectangles, 2½" x 3½"
   15 rectangles, 2½" x 6½"

From the cream solid, cut:
   10 squares, 3½" x 3½"

From the dark-gold solid, cut:
   20 strips, 1" x 6½"

Making the Blocks

1 Sew a 1½" x 3½" yellow rectangle to the top edge of a cream square. Sew a 2½" x 3½" yellow rectangle to the bottom edge of the square. Press the seam allowances toward the rectangles.

2 Sew a 2½" x 6½" yellow rectangle to the right side of the unit. Sew a 1½" x 6½" rectangle to the left side of the unit. Press the seam allowances toward the rectangles.

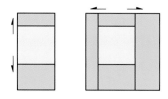

3 Measure and cut 2¾" from the left side of the assembled unit. Sew a dark-gold strip between the pieces of the unit. Press the seam allowances toward the strip.

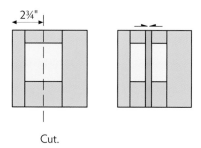

2¾"

Cut.

Sewing the Blocks

When inserting the dark gold strips, align the horizontal seam lines in the two sections and pin. The units can easily become skewed and will look wonky without care.

4 Rotate the unit 90°, positioning the dark-gold strip near the bottom edge, and cut again, 2¾" from the left side. Sew a dark-gold strip between the two pieces of the block. Press the seam allowances toward the dark-gold strip. Make 10, keeping the orientation of the pieced units the same when making each cut.

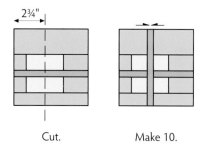

2¾"

Cut.   Make 10.

Straight Crosses

To add variety to the table runner, Jenifer chose to vary the measurements when she sliced the units before inserting the dark-gold strips. Use the photograph on page 27 as a guide to duplicate her free-form design, or cut all the units as directed for a more uniform appearance.

Assembling the Table Runner

1 Lay out the 10 blocks and the remaining 6½" yellow rectangles as shown or as desired. Rotate some blocks to vary the cross placement.

2 Sew the blocks and rectangles together in a row and press. The row should measure 6½" x 72½".

3 Sew the 5½" x 72½" yellow strip to one long edge of the pieced row. Sew the 1½" x 72½" yellow strip to the

other long edge. Press the seam allowances toward the strips.

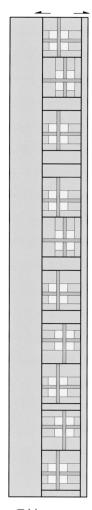

Table-runner assembly

Finishing the Table Runner

For more details on any of the finishing techniques, go to ShopMartingale.com /HowtoQuilt for free downloadable information.

1 Layer the table-runner top, batting, and 18" x 78" backing piece; baste the layers together. Quilt as desired.

2 Trim the backing and batting to match the table-runner top.

3 Join the 2" x 72" yellow strips and bind the table runner. Add a label if desired.

Reflected

A geometric table runner gives a modern look to your table. Use solid or tone-on-tone fabrics and let your quilting shine!

Designed and made by Angela Walters
Finished runner: 15" x 36" **Finished block:** 15" x 18"

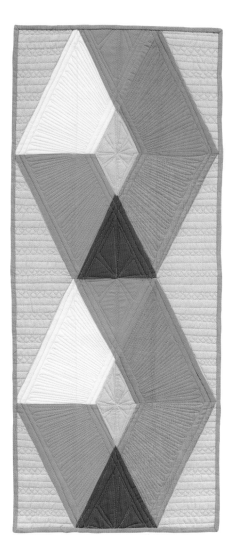

Materials

Yardage is based on 42"-wide fabric except as noted.

⅜ yard of cream solid for blocks

1 fat quarter *each* of light-green, chartreuse, light-blue, and light-teal solids for blocks

1 fat eighth of dark-teal solid for blocks

¼ yard of chartreuse solid for binding

⅝ yard of fabric for backing

21" x 42" piece of batting

Paper for foundation piecing

Cutting

All dimensions include ¼"-wide seam allowances. Refer to the cutting diagrams on page 30.

From the cream solid, cut:
> 2 rectangles, 5¾" x 11"; cut once diagonally as shown in diagram 1 to yield 4 triangles
> 2 rectangles, 5¾" x 11"; cut once diagonally as shown in diagram 2 to yield 4 triangles
> 8 rectangles, 2½" x 4"

From the light-green solid, cut:
> 1 rectangle, 5¾" x 11"; cut once diagonally as shown in diagram 1 to yield 2 triangles
> 2 rectangles, 4" x 10"

From the chartreuse solid, cut:
> 1 rectangle, 5¾" x 11"; cut once diagonally as shown in diagram 1 to yield 2 triangles
> 2 rectangles, 4" x 10"

From the light-blue solid, cut:
> 1 rectangle, 5¾" x 11; cut once diagonally as shown in diagram 2 to yield 2 triangles
> 2 rectangles, 4" x 10"
> 4 rectangles, 4" x 7"

Continued on page 31.

From the light-teal solid, cut:
  1 rectangle, 5¾" x 11"; cut once diagonally as shown in diagram 2 to yield 2 triangles
  2 rectangles, 4" x 10"

From the dark-teal solid, cut:
  4 rectangles, 4" x 7"

From the chartreuse solid for binding, cut:
  3 strips, 2½" x 42"

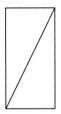

Cutting diagram 1   Cutting diagram 2

Making the Blocks

1 Assemble the half-rectangle triangles as shown to make eight rectangles, two each of four color combinations. Press the seam allowances toward the darker triangles. Trim each assembled rectangle to measure 5" x 9½".

Make 2 of each.

Foundation Piecing

Foundation piecing is an always-accurate method for assembling patchwork. Precise cutting and grain direction are less important than usual, and excess fabric is trimmed away after sewing. The basic steps are provided here, and you can find more information at ShopMartingale.com /HowtoQuilt.

1 Photocopy or trace the foundation patterns accurately onto copy paper. Roughly cut the foundations apart to separate the units.

2 Working with the printed side of the foundation on top, position a piece of fabric against the unprinted side of the foundation so it completely covers the area labeled 1. The wrong side of the fabric should lie against the foundation. Pin or glue baste this first patch to the foundation.

3 Position a second piece of fabric on the first, right sides together. The second patch should overlap the line between sections 1 and 2 on the foundation by at least ¼" and be positioned so that it will completely cover section 2 when the seam is sewn and the patches are pressed open. Holding the

foundation in front of a light source or a bright window helps reveal the lines as an aid to placement.

4 With the printed side of the foundation on top, sew directly on the line between sections 1 and 2. Use a shortened stitch length (1.6 mm to 1.8 mm) to facilitate removing the foundation later.

5 Trim the seam allowances of both patches to ¼" or slightly less. Do not cut the foundation. Fold patch 2 away from patch 1, smoothing it into position on the foundation, and press. Check to be sure sections 1 and 2 are completely covered with fabric, with at least ¼" seam allowances extending beyond the foundation lines.

6 Continue adding fabric patches until the foundation is completely covered. Baste the fabric to the foundation on or slightly outside of the foundation's outer seam line. Trim the foundation and fabric ¼" outside the seam line.

Foundations are usually left in place until a project is complete to ensure accuracy. To remove the foundations, hold each seam between your fingers to avoid distorting the stitches, and gently tear off the paper.

2 Make four copies of *each* pattern on page 33 for foundation piecing.

3 Referring to "Foundation Piecing" at right, use the patterns to make four of each unit, two in each color combination shown. Use the 4" x 10" rectangles in position 1, the 4" x 7" rectangles in position 2,

and the 2½" x 4" rectangles in position 3.

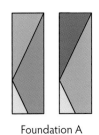

Foundation A   Foundation B

Make 2 of each.

Assembling the Table Runner

1 Referring to the block assembly diagram, make two blocks. Each block should measure 15½" x 18½".

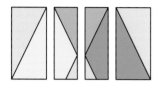

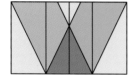

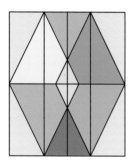

Make 2.

2 Sew the two blocks together along the 15½" edges to complete the table-runner top.

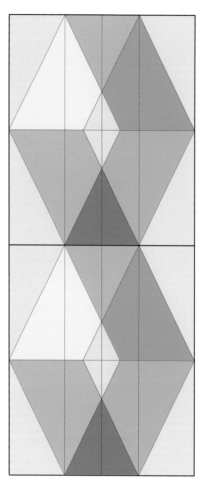

Table-runner assembly

3 Carefully remove the paper foundations and press the seam allowances open.

Make It Longer

If you need a longer table runner, simply make double the number of blocks.

Finishing the Table Runner

For more details on any of the finishing techniques, go to ShopMartingale.com /HowtoQuilt for free download-able information.

1 Layer the table-runner top, batting, and backing; baste the layers together. Quilt as desired.

2 Trim the backing and batting to match the table-runner top.

3 Join the 2½" x 42" char-treuse strips and bind the table runner. Add a label if desired.

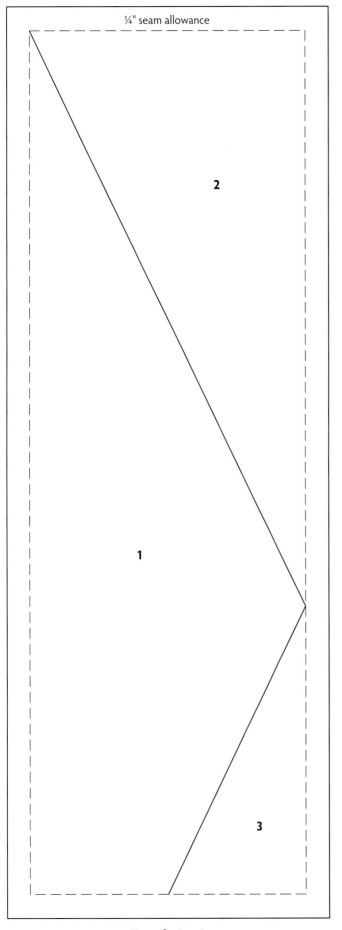

¼" seam allowance

2

1

3

Foundation A

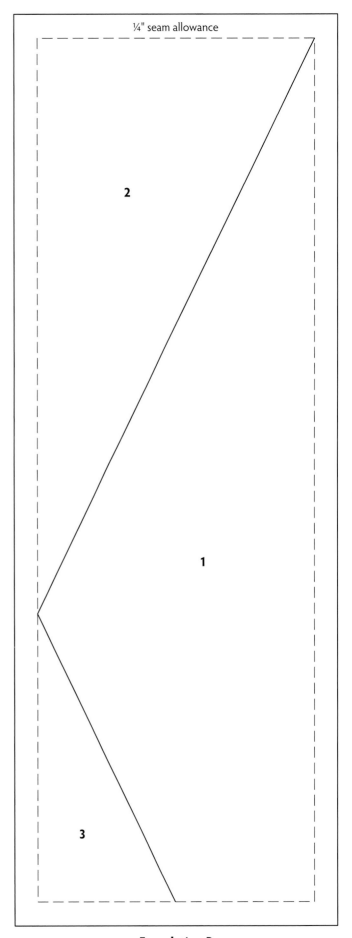

¼" seam allowance

2

1

3

Foundation B

Game Time

The design of this table runner relies on value contrasts more than print or color. Careful placement of lights and darks creates a checkerboard effect, giving the quilt a sense of fun and adding a feeling of complexity to a fairly simple project.

Designed and made by Candi Weinrick
Finished runner: 12" x 48"   Finished blocks: 8" x 8" and 8" x 10"

Materials

Yardage is based on 42"-wide fabric except as noted.

¼ yard of green solid for border

¼ yard of cream solid for border

1 fat eighth of dark-green solid for blocks*

1 fat eighth of light-peach solid for blocks*

1 fat eighth of bright-green solid for blocks*

1 fat eighth of peach solid for blocks*

1 fat eighth of light-green solid for blocks*

1 fat eighth of dark-peach solid for blocks*

⅓ yard of medium-brown solid for binding

¾ yard of fabric for backing

18" x 54" piece of batting

For this project, the fat eighths must measure at least 9" x 21". Substitute ¼-yard cuts if necessary.

Cutting

For easy assembly, keep the strips together in color pairs as you cut them. All dimensions include ¼"-wide seam allowances.

From *each* ¼ yard of green and cream solids, cut:
   5 strips, 1½" x 42"

From *each* of the dark-green and light-peach solids, cut:
   1 strip, 2½" x 21"

From *each* of the bright-green and peach solids, cut:
   2 strips, 2½" x 21"

From *each* of the light-green and dark-peach solids, cut:
   3 strips, 2½" x 21"

From the medium-brown solid, cut:
   4 strips, 2½" x 42"

Making the Blocks

Press the seam allowances in each strip set toward the darker color.

1 Sew the dark-green and light-peach strips together to create one strip set. Crosscut into eight segments, 2½" wide.

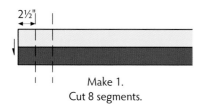

2½"

Make 1.
Cut 8 segments.

2 Sew a bright-green strip to each peach strip to make two strip sets. Crosscut into 16 segments, 2½" wide.

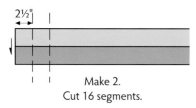

2½"

Make 2.
Cut 16 segments.

3 Sew a light-green strip to each dark-peach strip to make three strip sets. Crosscut into 20 segments, 2½" wide.

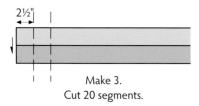

2½"

Make 3.
Cut 20 segments.

4 Join two units from step 1 to make a row; make four. Sew the four rows together to make a block, alternating colors as shown.

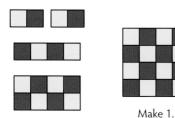

Make 1.

5 Repeat step 4 to make two blocks with the units from step 2, referring to the photo on page 35 for correct color placement. Then, join two units from step 3 to make a row; make 10. Sew five rows together to make a block, alternating colors as shown. Make two blocks.

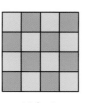
Make 2.

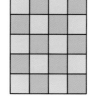
Make 2.

Making the Border

1 Sew a green strip to each cream strip to make five strip sets. Crosscut into 112 segments, 1½" wide.

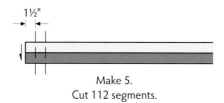

1½"

Make 5.
Cut 112 segments.

2 Stitch the units from step 1 together in pairs to create four-patch units; make 56.

Make 56.

3 Sew 22 four-patch units together to make a side border, paying careful attention to color placement as shown in the photograph. Make two. Sew six four-patch units together to make an end border; make two.

Assembling the Table Runner

1 Arrange the five checkerboard blocks as shown, with the dark-green/light-peach block in the center and the five-row blocks at each end. Sew the blocks together and press the seam allowances in one direction.

2 Sew a side border to each long edge of the runner. Stitch the end borders to the runner's short edges. Press the seam allowances toward the borders.

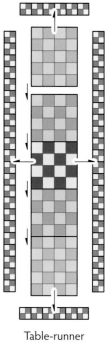

Table-runner
assembly

Finishing the Table Runner

For more details on any of the finishing techniques, go to ShopMartingale.com /HowtoQuilt for free downloadable information.

1 Cut two rectangles, 18" x 27", from the backing fabric. Sew the pieces together along the short edges; press the seam allowances open.

2 Layer the runner top, batting, and backing; baste the layers together. Quilt as desired.

3 Trim the backing and batting to match the table-runner top.

4 Join the 2½" x 42" medium-brown strips and bind the table runner. Add a label if desired.

Spring Blooms

This burst of spring will be a welcome addition to any table. Select beautiful floral fabrics that you love for your centerpiece, and you're on your way. This fast project makes a great last-minute gift, too!

Designed and pieced by Amy Ellis; quilted by Natalia Bonner
Finished runner: 13" x 38"   Finished block: 9" x 9"

Materials

Yardage is based on 42"-wide fabric except as noted.

¼ yard of white solid for blocks

1 fat quarter *each* of 3 floral prints for blocks

⅛ yard of yellow solid for blocks

½ yard of tan solid for setting triangles

⅓ yard of red floral for binding

¾ yard of fabric for backing

19" x 44" piece of batting

Cutting

All dimensions include ¼"-wide seam allowances.

From the white solid, cut:
   3 rectangles, 3" x 4½"
   3 rectangles, 2" x 3"
   6 squares, 2½" x 2½"
   12 squares, 2" x 2"

From *each* of the floral fat quarters, cut:
   1 square, 5½" x 5½"
   2 rectangles, 2½" x 4½"
   4 rectangles, 2" x 4½"

From the yellow solid, cut:
   3 squares, 2" x 2"

From the tan solid, cut:
   1 square, 13⅞" x 13⅞"; cut into quarters diagonally to yield
      4 triangles
   2 squares, 7¼" x 7¼"; cut in half diagonally to yield 4 triangles

From the red floral for binding, cut:
   3 strips, 2½" x 42"

Making the Blocks

1 Lightly draw a line from corner to corner on the wrong side of each 2" and 2½" white square.

2 Place a marked 2" square on one end of a 2" x 4½" floral-print rectangle, with right sides together and raw edges matching. Make two. Repeat with two more rectangles of the same floral print, arranging the drawn lines as shown. Repeat the process with two 2½" marked squares and two 2½" x 4½" floral rectangles of the same print.

Make 1.   Make 2.   Make 2.   Make 1.

3 Sew on each marked line. Trim the excess fabric ¼" outside the stitching line. Press the white triangles outward, pressing the seam allowances toward the triangles.

4 Arrange the units in two groups as shown. Sew each group together to create a flower-petal unit. Press the seam allowances in one direction.

 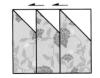

5 Repeat steps 2–4 to make a pair of flower-petal units from each of the three floral prints.

6 Sew a yellow square to each 2" x 3" white rectangle; make three. Press the seam allowances toward the yellow fabric. Sew a 3" x 4½" white rectangle to the right side of each unit.

7 Pin and sew one flower-petal unit to a matching floral-print square. Pin and sew the second flower-petal unit of the same print to the flower center, as shown. Press the seam allowances in opposite directions, and sew the block halves together. Make three, one of each floral print.

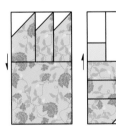

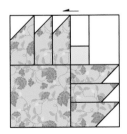

Make 3.

Assembling the Table Runner

1 Lay out the flower blocks and setting triangles as shown above right. Sew the triangles to the blocks in diagonal rows, and press the seam allowances toward the triangles.

2 Sew the rows together to complete the table runner. Press the seam allowances in one direction.

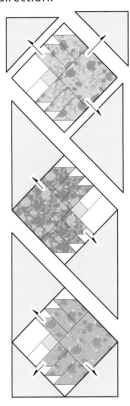

Table-runner assembly

Finishing the Table Runner

For more details on any of the finishing techniques, go to ShopMartingale.com /HowtoQuilt for free downloadable information.

1 Cut the backing fabric in half lengthwise. Sew the two pieces together along the short edges; press the seam allowances open.

2 Layer the runner top, batting, and backing; baste the layers together. Quilt as desired.

3 Trim the backing and batting to match the table-runner top.

4 Join the 2½" x 42" red-floral strips and bind the table runner. Add a label if desired.

Slices of Sunshine

W hat could be happier than cheerful slices of your favorite yellow prints? Pairing them with crisp white brings the clean, bright look of summer to your table. It's also a great opportunity to use up some of those scraps!

Designed and made by Jessica Levitt
Finished runner: 16½" x 62½"

Materials

Yardage is based on 42"-wide fabric except as noted.

¾ yard of white solid for patchwork

1 fat eighth *each* of 9 assorted yellow prints *OR* 18 scraps, *each* 9" x 10½", for patchwork

⅜ yard of yellow print for binding

1 yard of fabric for backing

22" x 68" piece of batting

Water-soluble fabric marker

Close Counts

If your yellow fabrics are a little small after squaring them, that's OK. The pieces can be a bit smaller, as long as each strip set has at least 10" of usable fabric. If you don't have 10", cut all the strip-set segments 2¼" wide; the table runner will be a little shorter but still look great.

Cutting

All dimensions include ¼"-wide seam allowances.

From the white solid, cut:
1 strip, 6" x 42"; crosscut into 3 rectangles, 6" x 10½"
1 strip, 7" x 42"; crosscut into 3 rectangles, 7" x 10½"
1 strip, 9" x 42"; crosscut into 3 rectangles, 9" x 10½"

From *each* of the yellow fat eighths, cut:
2 rectangles, 9" x 10½"

From the yellow print for binding, cut:
5 strips, 2¼" x 42"

Making the Strip Segments

1 On the right side of each white rectangle, mark a line along the lengthwise center with a removable fabric marker.

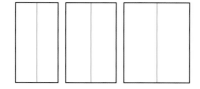

2 Sew a 9" x 10½" yellow rectangle to each 6" x 10½" white rectangle, using a different yellow print each time. Press the seam allowances toward the yellow fabric.

3 Sew a 9" x 10½" yellow rectangle to each 7" x 10½" white rectangle, again using a different yellow print each time. Press the seam allowances toward the yellow fabric.

4 Sew a 9" x 10½" yellow rectangle to each 9" x 10½" white rectangle, again using a different yellow print each time. Press the seam allowances toward the yellow fabric.

5 Sew a 9" x 10½" yellow rectangle to the opposite edge of each white rectangle from steps 2–4. Vary the prints used so that each unit includes two different yellows and no two prints are always paired with each other. Make nine.

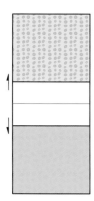

Make 9, 3 of each size.

6 Square one end of each unit from step 5, trimming it perpendicular to the seams. Crosscut each unit into four segments, 2½" wide, for a total of 36 segments. Five segments will be extra, allowing you a little added variety in arranging the runner top.

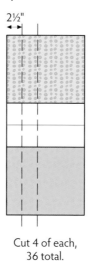

2½"

Cut 4 of each, 36 total.

The Long and Short of It

Jessica chose to use only 31 of the 36 strip segments to create her table runner, but you can make it up to 10" longer, if you wish, by using all of the segments.

Assembling the Table Runner

1 Prepare a design wall, table, or floor space by marking a center line 90" long with a piece of masking tape. Arrange 31 of the segments as shown, varying the placement of the yellow prints and the size of the white center sections. Center each fabric segment along the tape, using the marked lines on the white fabric as a guide. The strip lengths vary, so the outer edges will not align.

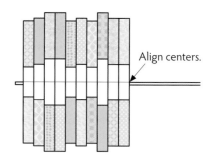

Align centers.

2 Once you are satisfied with the arrangement, move each segment off center by up to 3", shifting it either up or down. Move about the same number of segments in each direction, and don't end neighboring segments at the same spot. By shifting each segment no more than 3", you will maintain sufficient width for the table runner. Play with placement until the design looks sufficiently random to your eye.

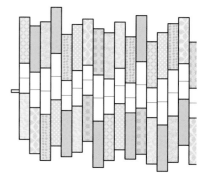

3 Without moving the strips, use the removable fabric marker to draw a line 8¼" from and parallel to the center line as shown. Trim with scissors or slide a cutting mat under the strips and trim along the line using a rotary cutter.

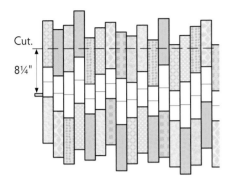

Cut.

8¼"

4 Sew the strips together in order, aligning the edges cut in step 3. Press the seam allowances in one direction.

5 Trim the remaining uneven edge of the runner so the width is 16½". Follow the manufacturer's instructions to remove all marked lines.

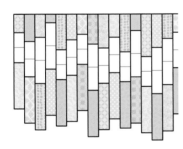

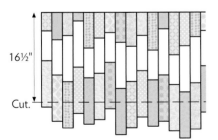

16½"

Cut.

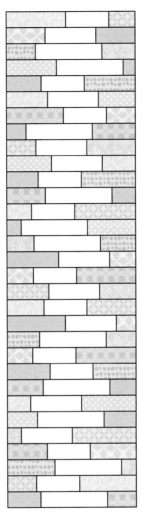

Table-runner assembly

Finishing the Table Runner

For more details on any of the finishing techniques, go to ShopMartingale.com /HowtoQuilt for free download-able information.

1 Cut the backing fabric in half lengthwise. Sew the two pieces together along the short edges; press the seam allowances open.

Scrappy Back

If you have extra segments, you can piece them into the backing to carry out the scrappy theme.

2 Layer the table-runner top, batting, and backing; baste the layers together. Quilt as desired.

3 Trim the backing and batting to match the table-runner top.

4 Join the 2¼" x 42" yellow-print strips and bind the table runner. Add a label if desired.

Chain Links

This modern table runner has extra-long dimensions so that it can hang over the ends of almost any dining table or sideboard. The simple, one-block design creates a fun, slightly off-balance look that highlights a few of your favorite fabrics. Choose high-contrast colors to add real "pop" to the length of your table.

Designed and made by Jessica Levitt
Finished runner: 13" x 120½" **Finished block: 8" x 12½"**

Materials
Yardage is based on 42"-wide fabric.

1⅛ yards of teal textural print for blocks

⅝ yard of green print for blocks

⅓ yard of orange print for blocks

½ yard of green solid for binding

1⅞ yards of fabric for backing

19" x 126" piece of batting

Cutting
All dimensions include ¼"-wide seam allowances.

From the teal textural print, cut:
1 strip, 4" x 42"; crosscut into 15 rectangles, 1¾" x 4"
3 strips, 5¼" x 42"; crosscut into 30 rectangles, 2¾" x 5¼"
2 strips, 8½" x 42"; crosscut into 15 rectangles, 3¾" x 8½"

From the green print, cut:
2 strips, 8½" x 42"; crosscut into 15 rectangles, 5" x 8½"

From the orange print, cut:
2 strips, 4" x 42"; crosscut into 15 squares, 4" x 4"

From the green solid, cut:
7 strips, 2¼" x 42"

Making the Blocks

1 Sew an orange square to a 1¾" x 4" teal rectangle. Press the seam allowances toward the darker fabric. Make 15.

Make 15.

2 Sew 2¾" x 5¼" teal rectangles to opposite sides of the unit. Press the seam allowances toward the darker fabric. Make 15.

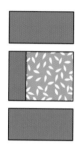 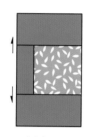

Make 15.

3 Sew a 3¾" x 8½" teal rectangle to one side of the unit from step 2 (against the orange square) and stitch a 5" x 8½" green rectangle to the opposite side. Press the seam allowances toward the darker fabrics. Make 15.

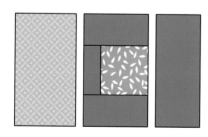

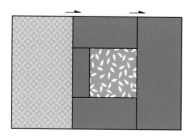

Make 15.

Assembling the Table Runner

1 Arrange the blocks as shown, rotating every other block.

Table-runner assembly

2 Sew the blocks together. Press the seam allowances in one direction.

Finishing the Table Runner

For more details on any of the finishing techniques, go to ShopMartingale.com /HowtoQuilt for free downloadable information.

1 Cut the backing fabric in half lengthwise. Sew the two pieces together along the short edges; press the seam allowances open.

2 Layer the table-runner top, batting, and backing; baste the layers together. Quilt as desired.

3 Trim the backing and batting to match the table-runner top.

4 Join the 2¼" x 42" green strips and bind the table runner. Add a label if desired.

About the Contributors

Natalie Barnes

Natalie is the owner of and designer for beyond the reef, a pattern-design company that she started in 1994 while drinking coffee on a lanai in Hanalei, Kauai. She learned to sew, knit, and crochet from her grandmother, and began quilting with 99-cent Woolworth fabrics. After a successful career in the demanding field of commercial interior design in Los Angeles, Natalie decided it was time to step out in faith, live her dream, and put her talents to work in another field. She has never looked back. Having always lived on the beach, she draws her inspiration from the sea, the sky, and the land. Natalie has lectured and taught quilt classes in Southern California, her quilts have been exhibited across the country, and her blog has developed an international readership. You can find her company online at beyondthereefpatterns.com, on Facebook, and, at times, on Twitter.

Audrie Bidwell

Born in Singapore and reared in Australia, Audrie found quilting after she moved to the United States. Quilting was the perfect outlet for her creativity and has led her to a community she's proud to be part of. She doesn't come from a crafty family, but she taught herself to sew and knit. She still can't draw to save her life. Audrie loves working with bright colors and draws inspiration from traditional designs. She lives in Connecticut with her husband and two Ragdoll kitties. She can be found online at BlueIsBleu.blogspot.com, where she chronicles her life and loves.

Josée Carrier

Josée has worked in the engineering field and is currently a stay-at-home mom. In her free time, you can find her in her sewing room. She loves creating with fabrics and threads and designing projects of her own. In quilting and patchwork projects she has found a great way to express her creativity. She is part of the Modern Quilt Guild and cofounder of its Montreal branch. To learn more about her projects, visit her at TheCharmingNeedle.com.

Jenifer Dick

Jenifer began quilting in 1993 when, on a whim, she signed up for a beginning quiltmaking class. From the moment she finished that first wall hanging, she was hooked. The author of several quilting books, Jenifer appreciates all aspects of quiltmaking, from researching historical quilts and contemporary art quilts to traditional and modern quilting. She lives in Harrisonville, Missouri, with her husband and three children. You can follow her on her blog at 42Quilts.com.

Amy Ellis

Amy was amazed to discover the great source of inspiration and abundance of knowledge that is the blogging world, and decided to become a part of it. Via Amy's Creative Side, she shares current projects (including quilts, bags, and the occasional garment), product reviews, and little bits of her family life as a wife and mom to four. She hosts a biannual Bloggers' Quilt Festival of inspiring quilts and stories; there's no judging or required skill set for entry, so it's more like a big party online! Amy is the author of two books and this is her third time as a contributor. Visit her at AmysCreativeSide.com.

Heather Jones

Heather is a designer and modern quilter. She lives in Cincinnati with her husband, Jeff, and two young children, Aidan and Olivia, who are her biggest supporters as well as her greatest sources of inspiration. Heather founded the Cincinnati chapter of the Modern Quilt Guild and recently completed her first line of quilting patterns. Three of her original quilts were chosen as winners of the Modern Quilt Guild's Project Modern Challenges, a yearlong national quilting competition. For more information on Heather and her work, please visit her blog at OliveAndOllie.com.

Thomas Knauer

Thomas holds masters of fine art degrees from both Ohio University and the Cranbrook Academy of Art. Before he started designing fabric and quilts, he was a professor of art and design at Drake University and the State University of New York. He began sewing in 2010 after leaving the academic life due to health concerns; the first time he sat down at a sewing machine, he made his wee daughter a dress. Thomas now designs fabric with Andover Fabrics, and his quilts are being published in an array of magazines. He still loves making things for his wee daughter.

Jessica Levitt

Jessica has been sewing and quilting since the age of 12. Always thirsting for some new craft, she has taught herself countless quilting techniques, as well as clothing and costume design, event design, and home decor. She is also the author of a sewing-project book and has designed several lines of fabric for Windham Fabrics. Her degree in electrical engineering from Duke University now goes largely unused while she pursues more creative endeavors. Jessica lives and works in New Jersey with her husband and two beautiful children. You can see her latest projects and catch up on her life at her blog, Juicy-Bits.typepad.com.

Angela Walters

Angela is a long-arm quilter, teacher, and the author of two books about quiltmaking. Her quilting career began at the side of her husband's grandfather, and together they made her first quilt. Thousands of swirls, feathers, and parallel lines later, she has turned her love of stitches and fabric into a thriving business focused on modern machine quilting. Angela lives on the outskirts of Kansas City, Missouri, with her husband, three children, and many, many quilts. Learn more about her and her love of quilting at QuiltingIsMyTherapy.com.

Candi Weinrick

Candi started quilting when she and two friends stumbled upon a quilt shop, and it's been love ever since. She believes every quilt should include solid fabrics and considers her style to be traditional with a modern edge. You can visit her website, RaccoonCreekQuilts.com, where she blogs about sewing "hits and misses." Occasionally her daughter hijacks her blog to add witty cartoons and beg for another quilt.